Spelling

GW01179896

AGE 9-11

Angela Burt

Illustrated by Alan Rowe

Some children are naturally good spellers but many others need a helping hand. It is hoped that this workbook will provide the necessary help and guidance in a practical and enjoyable way.

The approach has been a systematic one, dealing with spelling rules and patterns which are the key to thousands of otherwise troublesome words in daily use. Spellings that have to be learned by heart because they don't follow rules are also included and advice is given on how to learn them.

The reinforcement exercises and word puzzles are meant to be fun to do as well as being educationally sound. It should be possible to get all the answers right all the time if care is taken and this regular success will build confidence as nothing else can.

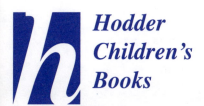

Hodder Children's Books

NATIONAL CONFEDERATION OF · PARENT TEACHER ASSOCIATIONS ·

The only home learning programme supported by the NCPTA

How to help your child

● **Arrange regular sessions of about 20 minutes.** It is better to have three or four short sessions a week than long sessions at irregular intervals.

● **Praise and encourage wherever possible.** Build your child's confidence by stressing the positive at all times. Praise even partial success.

● **Be available as your child tackles new topics.** Your child may want to work independently but there are times when you can help to reinforce a rule by repeating it or helping with the pronunciation of a word that has to be learned by heart. Be sensitive to your child's desire to be in control – self-motivation is very valuable – but be available when needed. You might reserve for yourself the role of marker. The answers are at the back of the book.

● **Encourage your child to keep a spelling notebook.** Instructions for making an inexpensive spelling notebook are on the opposite page. All words which your child is likely to need often and is unsure of should be stored in the notebook for easy reference.

● **Ensure your child has a suitable dictionary.** Children outgrow dictionaries very rapidly but will not yet be ready for an adult dictionary. School, bookshop and library will all be able to advise you. The National Curriculum encourages the use of suitable reference books and a dictionary is indispensable.

ISBN 0 340 72651 2
Text copyright © 1998 Angela Burt
Illustrations copyright © 1998 Alan Rowe

The rights of Angela Burt and Alan Rowe to be identified
as the author and illustrator of this work have been asserted by them
in accordance with the Copyright, Designs and Patents Act 1988.

First published in Great Britain 1998

Printed in Great Britain

10 9 8 7 6 5 4 3
Published by Hodder Children's Books, a division of Hodder Headline plc, 338 Euston Road, London NW1 3BH.

A CIP record is registered by and held at the British Library.

How to make a spelling notebook

Buy or make an indexed notebook that will fit into your pocket or bag. Use it at school and at home to find quickly words you often need to look up.

You need at least 26 pages. Extra pages at the end are useful for lists.

26 tabs. If notebook is at least 13 cm long, you can allow $\frac{1}{2}$ cm of each tab to show.

Draw a line down the middle of each page.

Label tabs alphabetically: A B C D E F G H I J K L M N O P Q R S T U V W X Y Z.

How to learn a spelling by heart

LOOK   Really look at the word. Take a mental photograph. Notice how it's put together. Spot anything <u>unusu</u>al.

SAY   Say the word aloud. Sometimes it helps to say each letter separately (w - h - o); sometimes it helps to stress each syllable (Wed - nes - day).

COVER   When you're ready, cover the word. Don't cheat.

WRITE   Write the whole word from memory. Say the word aloud as you write.

CHECK   Now check and see how you've got on. If you've made a mistake, **look** very carefully to see exactly where you've gone wrong, then say, cover, write and check once again. You may have to do this several times but in the end you'll learn the word for ever!

Silent letters

Read these words aloud. Be very careful not to pronounce the silent letters but notice where they are.

b	c	g	gh	h	k
lam**b**	s**c**enery	**g**nash	li**gh**t	**h**onest	**k**nee
lim**b**	s**c**ience	**g**naw	dau**gh**ter	**g**host	**k**not
de**b**t	mus**c**le	si**g**n	dou**gh**nut	**g**herkin	**k**nuckle

knight

gnome

Can you spell me?

1 I cut food. | nife

2 I mend pipes. | plum er

3 I live next door. | nei bour

4 I cut paper. | s issors

5 I bite you. | nat

6 I can be cooked. | r ubarb

Use letters from the circle to complete these words.

7 umb

8 sign

9 aight

10 reign

11 kno

12 wro

Circle: n, fo, ck, de, str, ng

4

More silent letters

Read these words aloud. Notice where the silent letters are.

n	p	w
solem**n**	**p**salm	**w**rap
colum**n**	ras**p**berry	**w**rite
autum**n**	recei**p**t	s**w**ord

t	u
lis**t**en	g**u**ide
cas**t**le	g**u**itar
mis**t**letoe	g**u**ilty

He's got a silent letter too!

pterodactyl

Can you spell me?

1 I'm the smallest bird in Britain.   w

2 I'm a rodent without a tail.   g   -p

3 I join your hand and arm.   w

4 I am sung in church.   h

5 I am someone who is invited.   g

Dictionary search.   Use your dictionary to track down the missing letters.

6 *pseu _ _ _ _ _*   **7** *guill _ _ _ _ _*   **8** *wr _ a _ _*

Learn these words by heart.
Ask someone to test you
when you are ready.
Enter your score in the box.

moment   tomorrow
Tuesday   Wednesday
Saturday

*These are words
you often need.
Try to get all of
them right.*

SCORE

5

Homophones (sound-alikes)

same sound   different meaning   different spelling

hear	Can you **hear** me at the back?
here	**Here** it is. Over **here**! (= place)
its	The dog wagged **its** tail.
it's	**It's** not fair. (= it is)
know	Do you **know** the answer?
no	**No**, I have **no** idea.
their	They have lost **their** cat.
there	**There** is a present for everyone over **there**. (= place)
they're	**They're** moving to London. (= they are)
to	Everyone wants **to** come **to** my party.
too	I've eaten **too** much. (= more than enough) You have **too**. (= as well)
two	Bicycles have **two** wheels.

Use these examples to help you WRITE the RIGHT spellings every time!

You HEAR with your EAR.

***were**	(rhymes with 'her')	We **were** hoping you would win.
***we're**	(rhymes with 'ear')	**We're** very pleased. (= we are)
***where**	(rhymes with 'air')	**Where** is my shirt? (= place)

here
th**ere**   all refer to places
wh**ere**

who's	**Who's** afraid of ghosts? (= who is)
whose	**Whose** shoebag is this?
your	Have you done **your** homework?
you're	**You're** a good friend. (= you are)

* These don't have exactly the same sound, but are often confused.

Tick the right word.

1. The girls [were] [we're] [where] having a test.
2. Would you like [to] [too] [two] come with us?
3. There's [know] [no] point in cheating.
4. Try not [to] [too] [two] lose [your] [you're] temper.
5. Wait for me [hear] [here] .
6. [Its] [It's] nearly four o'clock.

Look at the examples on the opposite page for help.

Use words from the circle to fill the blanks.

no
know here
hear we're
where
were

7. [   ] [   ] you this morning?
8. I [   ] I have [   ] chance of winning.
9. [   ] sorry that [   ] late.
10. I couldn't [   ] a sound.
11. Do you [   ] my middle name?
12. I can guess [   ] they are.

Choose the right word from the brackets.

13. You [   ] supposed to lay the table. (we're / were / where)
14. [   ] both good at basketball. (Their / There / They're)
15. [   ] not allowed to eat in the computer room. (Your / You're)
16. [   ] your turn next. (Its / It's)
17. I can [   ] someone coming. (hear / here)

LOOK   SAY   COVER   WRITE   CHECK

Learn these words by heart.
Ask someone to test you
when you are ready.
Enter your score in the box.

across   among
paid   perhaps
something

SCORE
/ 5

■ TEST 1 ■

Silent letters

Fill in the missing letters.

❶	nife	❽	si n	⓯	g itar
❷	s issors	❾	mus le	⓰	recei t
❸	de t	❿	onest	⓱	rist
❹	g ost	⓫	solem	⓲	g est
❺	nee	⓬	dau ter	⓳	hym
❻	s ience	⓭	s ord	⓴	reath
❼	nuckle	⓮	rite		

Homophones

Tick the word that is needed in each sentence.

㉑ | Its | It's | very hot today.

㉒ My cat is | to | too | two | lazy to hunt mice.

㉓ They | were | we're | where | helping to pick apples.

㉔ | Their | There | They're | always late on Mondays.

㉕ I don't | know | no | Anne's phone number.

㉖ | Your | You're | very kind.

㉗ Did you | hear | here | thunder in the night?

Learn-by-heart spellings

Put a circle around the correct spelling.

㉘ | paid | payed | paied |

㉙ | amoung | among | ammong |

㉚ | perhaps | prehaps | pepraps |

Score one point for each correct answer.

8

Apostrophes in contractions

We use apostrophes **'** to show where letters have been left out
in shortened words.

Here are some examples. There are lots more.

I'm	= I am	**don't**	= do not
you're	= you are	**can't**	= cannot
what's	= what is / what has	**won't**	= will not
it's	= it is / it has	**shan't**	= shall not
we'll	= we will / we shall	**didn't**	= did not
we've	= we have	**couldn't**	= could not
could've	= could have	**isn't**	= is not

Write the shortened form in the second half of each of the boxes below.

1 She [**cannot**] believe it.

2 It [**is not**] fair.

3 I [**have not**] asked them.

4 They [**did not**] reply.

5 [**I am**] sure that

[**you are**] wrong.

6 You [**should have**] told your parents.

7 They [**will not**] guess the answer.

Can you spot the difference?

did'nt ✗   didn't ✓
is'nt ✗   isn't ✓

LOOK   SAY   COVER   WRITE   CHECK

Learn these words by heart.
Ask someone to test you
when you are ready.
Enter your score in the box.

excited   favourite
intelligent   lonely
necessary

SCORE

5

Prefixes (word beginnings)

Prefixes are added to the beginnings of words.

A lot of prefixes come from Latin and Greek, and can be hard to spell. If you learn the prefixes, you'll have learned the hardest part of hundreds of words.

Here are some examples. There are lots more.

anti– (against)   **anti**climax, **anti**septic
auto– (self)   **auto**matic, **auto**graph
fore– (in advance/in front)   **fore**cast, **fore**ground
inter– (between)   **inter**national, **Inter**net
micro– (small)   **micro**chip, **micro**scope
tele– (at a distance)   **tele**vision, **tele**scope

Prefixes help you understand the meanings of words.

Use the prefixes above to complete these words.

1   biography   3   phone   5   wave
2   freeze   4   view   6   tell

Opposites

Use these prefixes to make opposites: **in–   un–   dis–   mis–**

Here are some examples.

invisible   **in**numerable
unhappy   **un**natural
disappear   **dis**sect
misunderstand   **mis**spell

Can you see why words in this column have double letters?

Notice how **in–** changes sometimes:

ignorant   **il**legal   **im**mortal
impossible   **ir**responsible

Use the prefixes above to complete these words.

7   certain   10   polite   13   replaceable
8   behave   11   direct   14   connect
9   agree   12   conscious   15   helpful

Suffixes (word endings)

Suffixes are added to the end of words.

Here are some examples.

dark**ness**   friend**ship**   keen**ness**

king**dom**   appoint**ment**   loca**lly**

comfort**able**   use**less**   usua**lly**

Here is a really useful tip!

Whenever FULL is used as a suffix, it is spelled –ful.

Here are some examples: care**ful**   help**ful**   success**ful**   wonder**ful**   spoon**ful**

Now add **–ly**: **careful + ly = carefully.**

Spell these word sums:

1 kind + ness =

2 friend + ly =

3 exist + ence =

4 final + ly =

5 joy + full =

6 sad + ness =

7 especial + ly =

8 play + full + ly =

Some suffixes come in sound-alike pairs and groups. When in doubt which one to use, look in your dictionary.

Choose the right spelling and write it in the box.

9 visable or visible?

10 grammar or grammer?

11 sentance or sentence?

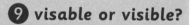

Write words you need a lot in your spelling notebook.

LOOK   SAY   COVER   WRITE   CHECK

Learn these words by heart.
Ask someone to test you
when you are ready.
Enter your score in the box.

description   disappearance
disease   safety
sentence

SCORE
5

■ TEST 2 ■

Apostrophes   Write the short form using the apostrophe.

1 we have _____   **5** do not _____   **8** should have _____

2 they are _____   **6** shall not _____   **9** I will _____

3 who has _____   **7** did not _____   **10** it has _____

4 are not _____

Prefixes   Use prefixes to make these words opposite in meaning.

11 understand   **14** legible   **17** behave

12 known   **15** agree   **18** regular

13 approve   **16** possible

Suffixes   Spell these word sums.

19 immediate + ly   **21** forget + full   **23** wonder + full + ly

= _____   = _____   = _____

20 advertise + ment   **22** sullen + ness

= _____   = _____

Circle the correct spelling.

24   visable   visible   **26**   careful   carefull

25   realy   really   **27**   keeness   keenness

Learn-by-heart spellings

Write out the correct spellings in the spaces provided.

28 exited   excited   exsited   _____

29 describtion   description   discription   _____

30 lonely   lonly   lonley   _____

Score one point for each correct answer.

SCORE

/30

Plurals

SINGULAR means ONE of something	**PLURAL** means MORE THAN ONE

Add **–s** to make most words plural.

three cat|**s**   two boy|**s**   twenty chair|**s**

Add **–es** to words ending in these sounds:

s	**x**	**z**	**ch**	**sh**	**tch**

glass|**es** fox|**es** fez|**es** lunch|**es** dish|**es** match|**es**

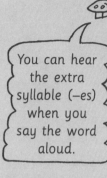

You can hear the extra syllable (–es) when you say the word aloud.

Make these words plural.

1 pencil   **5** brush

2 address   **6** box

3 crutch   **7** peach

4 blackboard   **8** ruler   **9** prefix

Write the plurals of these words.

10 princess

11 argument

12 sentence

13 suffix

14 examination

15 business

16 advertisement

Say the word aloud.

LOOK	SAY	COVER	WRITE	CHECK

Learn these words by heart.
Ask someone to test you
when you are ready.
Enter your score in the box.

**annoyed   different
expensive   immediately
recently**

SCORE

/ 5

13

Plurals of –y words

key

keys

cherry

cherries

The plural of key is key**s**. The plural of cherry is cherr**ies**. Do you know the rule for making –y words plural? It's very useful because there are NO EXCEPTIONS. It works every time.

Words ending in a **vowel** + **y** (like key) add **–s** for the plural.

Words ending in a **consonant** + **y** (like cherry) change **y** to **–ies**.

Now use the rule to make these words plural.

Remember there are five vowels: a, e, i, o and u.

1 jockey

2 monkey

3 trolley

4 birthday

5 butterfly

6 baby

7 party

8 lorry

Change these plural words back to the singular.

9 robberies

10 alleys

11 jellies

12 daisies

13 journeys

14 memories

Turn the words in brackets into the plural.

15 The new office block has sixteen (storey).

16 The Welsh (valley) are very beautiful.

17 We heard (cry) for help.

18 (Bully) are cowards at heart.

19 My sister has so many different (allergy).

20 The (donkey) had been badly treated.

Plurals of –o words

piano   pianos

Musical –o words add –s in the plural.
piano|**s**   banjo|**s**   soprano|**s**

All –o words from Spanish add –s in the plural.
sombrero|**s**   poncho|**s**   bronco|**s**

All shortened words ending in –o add –s in the plural.
disco|**s** (from discothèque)   photo|**s** (from photograph)
kilo|**s** (from kilogramme / kilogram)

All –o words ending in two vowels add –s in the plural.
cameo|**s**   radio|**s**   kangaroo|**s**

Take care with the words that must be –es.

cargo**es**		
domino**es**	mosquito**es**	tornado**es**
echo**es**	potato**es**	torpedo**es**
hero**es**	tomato**es**	volcano**es**

Make these words plural.

1 tattoo

2 video

3 tomato

4 studio

5 contralto

6 potato

7 patio

8 echo

9 cuckoo

LOOK   SAY   COVER   WRITE   CHECK

Learn these words by heart.
Ask someone to test you
when you are ready.
Enter your score in the box.

anxious   awkward
difficult   jealous
ridiculous

SCORE

5

More plurals (f words)

sheriff

sheriffs

knife

knives

QUESTION: How can you tell when you have to add –s and when you have to change –f or –fe to –ves?

ANSWER: You just have to say the plural word aloud. You can HEAR when it's –ves.

Usually add –s to make –f words plural.

sheriff**s**   cliff**s**   chief**s**   handkerchief**s**   roof**s**

Learn the 13 words that are –ves in the plural.

elf ➡ el**ves**	leaf ➡ lea**ves**	wolf ➡ wol**ves**
self ➡ sel**ves**	sheaf ➡ shea**ves**	life ➡ li**ves**
shelf ➡ shel**ves**	thief ➡ thie**ves**	knife ➡ kni**ves**
calf ➡ cal**ves**	loaf ➡ loa**ves**	wife ➡ wi**ves**
half ➡ hal**ves**		

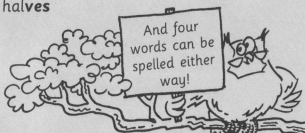

And four words can be spelled either way!

hoofs or hooves
scarfs or scarves
turfs or turves
wharfs or wharves

Make these words plural.

1 belief ⬜   **3** wife ⬜   **5** loaf ⬜

2 roof ⬜   **4** cuff ⬜   **6** hoof ⬜

Put a circle around the correct spelling.

7 themselfs   themselves

8 proofs   prooves

9 leafs   leaves

10 reefs   reeves

Remember! Say the words aloud and you'll **hear** the right spelling.

Peculiar plurals

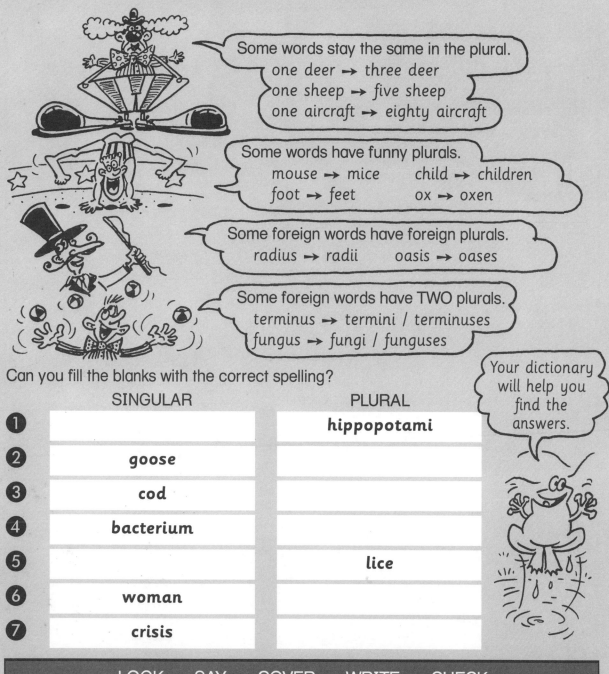

Some words stay the same in the plural.
one deer → three deer
one sheep → five sheep
one aircraft → eighty aircraft

Some words have funny plurals.
mouse → mice   child → children
foot → feet   ox → oxen

Some foreign words have foreign plurals.
radius → radii   oasis → oases

Some foreign words have TWO plurals.
terminus → termini / terminuses
fungus → fungi / funguses

Can you fill the blanks with the correct spelling?

Your dictionary will help you find the answers.

	SINGULAR	PLURAL
1		hippopotami
2	goose	
3	cod	
4	bacterium	
5		lice
6	woman	
7	crisis	

LOOK   SAY   COVER   WRITE   CHECK

Learn these words by heart.
Ask someone to test you
when you are ready.
Enter your score in the box.

definitely   extremely
scarcely   separately
sincerely

SCORE

5

Add **–s** or **–es**

1. station   3. cross   5. computer
2. telephone   4. match   6. stitch

Make these –y words plural.

7. hobby   10. memory
8. key   11. story
9. century   12. storey

Make these –o words plural.

13. disco   15. tomato   17. volcano
14. echo   16. piano   18. igloo

Make these –f words plural.

19. roof   22. handerchief
20. half   23. shelf
21. belief   24. flagstaff

Make these words plural.

25. child   28. mouse
26. deer   29. ox
27. oasis   30. woman

Score one point
for each
correct answer.

SCORE

/ 30

■ TEST 3 PART 2 ■

Mixed plurals. Make these words plural.

1 fox

2 wolf

3 louse

4 lynx

5 trout

6 kangaroo

7 turkey

8 walrus

9 canary

10 lioness

11 hen

12 pony

13 wallaby

14 stag

15 goose

16 cockatoo

Make these words singular.

17 hooves

18 enemies

19 cargoes

20 kimonos

21 fungi

Learn-by-heart spellings. Circle the correct spellings.

22 seperately separatly separately

23 imediately immediately immeadiately

24 scarsley scarsely scarcely

25 difficult differcult difficalt

26 exstreamly extreamly extremely

27 definately deffinatly definitely

28 anxious angshous anksious

29 sincerly sincerely sincerly

30 annoied anoyed annoyed

Score one point each

LOOK   SAY   COVER   WRITE   CHECK

Learn these words by heart.
Ask someone to test you
when you are ready.
Enter your score in the box.

**address   decision
embarrassment
opportunity   suggestion**

1 – 1 – 1

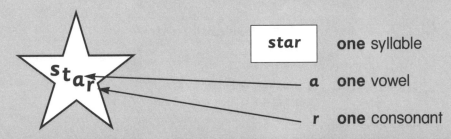

star	**one** syllable
a	**one** vowel
r	**one** consonant

| – | – | words are words of ONE syllable ending in ONE vowel + ONE consonant.

mop   pin   mat   tap   step   shop

Find the three | – | – | words in the list below.
Tick the | – | – | words and cross out the others.

look	hint	chair
sin	sink	fun
crack	clip	

Take care when you add suffixes to | – | – | words.

■   Double the final letter (except w, x, y) before adding a suffix beginning with a vowel.

blot + ed = blot|t|ed   pin + ing = pin|n|ing

■   Don't double the final letter before adding a suffix beginning with a consonant.

sin + ful = sinful   mad + ness = madness

Add these vowel suffixes to these | – | – | words.

❶ snap + ing

❷ sad + en

❸ fun + y

Y counts as a vowel at the end of a word. It **sounds** like e then.

Add these consonant suffixes to these | – | – | words.

❹ sad + ly   ❻ fret + ful

❺ spot + less

Add these mixed endings to 1-1-1 words.

1 drag + ing

2 rim + less

3 win + er

4 pig + let

5 wrap + er

6 sun + y

7 scar + ed

8 drop + let

Be careful. Look at the rule again if you've forgotten it.

In this wordsearch look for 1-1-1 words with vowel and consonant endings.

9 _ _ _ _ _ **ed**

10 _ _ _ _ _ **ed**

11 _ _ _ _ _ **er**

12 _ _ _ **ness**

13 _ _ _ **ness**

13 _ _ _ **ly**

15 _ _ _ **ly**

s	n	a	p	p	e	d
w	a	q	n	a	y	i
e	r	d	f	t	l	m
t	b	a	n	t	d	n
t	b	o	k	e	a	e
e	h	u	v	d	s	s
r	y	l	t	o	h	s

LOOK   SAY   COVER   WRITE   CHECK

Learn these words by heart.
Ask someone to test you
when you are ready.
Enter your score in the box.

apology   **argument**
college   **luxury**
opinion

SCORE

/ 5

Magic –e

Say these words aloud: hop plan win

Now add magic –e and say them again:

That's magic!

Now we'll add suffixes to magic –e words and you'll see some more magic.

Drop the magic –e when you add a vowel suffix.
  hope + ing = hoping

Keep the magic –e when you add a consonant suffix.
  hope + less = hopeless

Add these vowel suffixes to these magic –e words.

1 **make + ing**

2 **fame + ous**

3 **laze + y**

Add these consonant suffixes to these magic –e words.

4 **safe + ly**

5 **sincere + ly**

6 **some + thing**

And magic –e GOES ON WORKING whether it's still there or not. Say **hoping** and **hopeless** aloud!

Add these mixed suffixes to these magic –e words.

7 **tire + some**

8 **excite + ing**

9 **value + able**

10 **announce + ment**

truly   wholly   whilst
duly   awful   width
ninth   wisdom
argument

But remember these exceptions. You'd expect them to keep –e and they don't!

And remember to keep the –e and not drop it in:
noticeable courageous
gorgeous outrageous

And keep the –e in funny words like dyeing (not the same as dying!) and singeing (not the same as singing!)

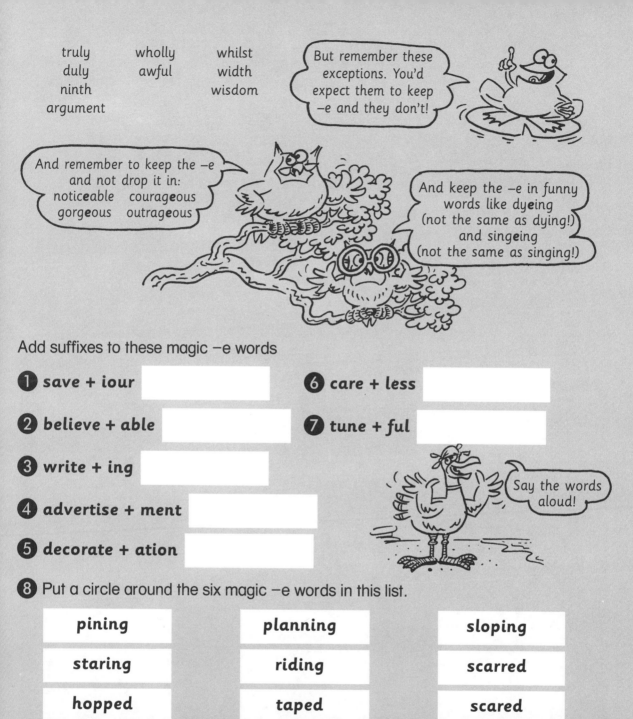

Add suffixes to these magic –e words

1 save + iour

2 believe + able

3 write + ing

4 advertise + ment

5 decorate + ation

6 care + less

7 tune + ful

Say the words aloud!

8 Put a circle around the six magic –e words in this list.

pining	planning	sloping
staring	riding	scarred
hopped	taped	scared

Y words

Do you remember the rule for adding plural endings to −y words (page 14):

It's much the same when you add other endings like −able, −ing, −ous, −ful, −ment and −ness.

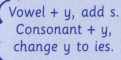

Vowel + y, add s.
Consonant + y, change y to ies.

If the base word ends in vowel + y, just add suffix.

base word

enjoy + able = enjoyable

enjoy + ing = enjoying

enjoy + ment = enjoyment

If the base word ends in consonant + y, change y to i before adding suffix (unless suffix already begins with i).

bury + al = burial   (but bury + ing = burying)

glory + ous = glorious

mercy + ful = merciful

Add these suffixes to vowel + y words.

1 employ + ment

2 delay + ed

3 betray + al

Add these suffixes to consonant + y words.

4 copy + er

5 beauty + ful

6 empty + ness

7 forty + eth

8 worry + ing

Now try adding suffixes to both kinds of −y words on the next page.

Add these suffixes to both kinds of —y words.

1 funny + est _____

6 mystery + ous _____

2 terrify + ing _____

7 deny + al _____

3 early + er _____

8 worry + ed _____

4 delay + ing _____

9 lazy + est _____

5 baby + ish _____

10 play + full _____

What am I? Unjumble me.

11 rrrcaei   a _____ bag

12 yrarpe   a heartfelt _____

13 mnpyate   a late _____

There are just a few exceptions to the rule.
Learn them by heart.

daily	babyhood
gaily	shyly
laid	shyness
paid	dryness
said	

Learn these words by heart.
Ask someone to test you
when you are ready.
Enter your score in the box.

gradually   handkerchief
recognise or **recognize**
library   sandwich

SCORE

/ 5

2 – 1 – 1

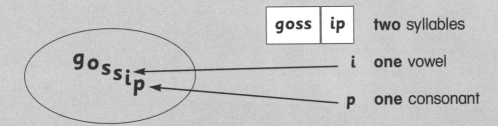

goss	ip	**two** syllables

gossip

i **one** vowel

p **one** consonant

> 2–1–1 words are words of TWO syllables ending in
> ONE vowel + ONE consonant.

Say **gossip**, **happen** and **market** out loud.
Notice that in these 2–1–1 words you stress
the <u>first</u> syllable.

adMIT
forGET
eQUIP
2

GOSSip
HAPPen
MARket
1

Now say **admit**, **forget** and **equip** out loud.
Notice that in these 2–1–1 words you stress
the <u>second</u> syllable.

Now LISTen
to the rule.

And don't
forGET it!

No change to the base word when you add a consonant suffix.

    forget + ful = forgetful   equip + ment = equipment

No change to the base word when you add a vowel suffix IF THE STRESS IS
ON THE FIRST SYLLABLE.

    gossip + ing = gossiping   happen + ed = happened

Double the last letter of the base word when you add a vowel suffix IF THE STRESS
IS ON THE SECOND SYLLABLE.

    forget + ing = forgetting   admit + ed = admitted

Add these consonant suffixes.

1 number + less

2 shatter + proof

3 gossip + monger

Add these vowel suffixes.

4 rivet + ing

5 differ + ence

6 orbit + ed

7 submit + ed

8 forbid + en

9 equip + ing

Never double w, x, y.
allowed
relaxed
delayed

Always double kidnap and worship.
kidnapped
worshipped

2-1-1 words ending in –l

These are a special case. They USUALLY double before a vowel suffix (labelled, cancellation, quarrelling) but there are exceptions. Check in a dictionary if in doubt.

Dictionary search. One *l* or two?

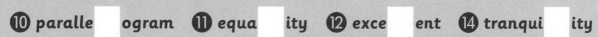

10 paralle___ogram **11** equa___ity **12** exce___ent **14** tranqui___ity

LOOK   SAY   COVER   WRITE   CHECK

Learn these words by heart.
Ask someone to test you
when you are ready.
Enter your score in the box.

burglar   government
information
secretary   surprised

SCORE

/5

■ TEST 4 ■

1–1–1 and magic –e   Add these suffixes.

1 hop + ing

3 sun + y

5 excite + ment

2 hope + ing

4 mad + ly

6 some + thing

Y words   Add these suffixes.

7 worry + ed

9 obey + ing

11 twenty + eth

8 noisy + ly

10 vary + ous

12 enjoy + ment

2–1–1   Add these suffixes.

13 gossip + ed

15 commit + ed

17 follow + er

14 regret + ful

16 happen + ing

18 label + ed

Mixed exercise   Do these word sums.

19 lazy + ness
=

22 hope + less
=

25 gallop + ing
=

20 slope + ing
=

23 easy + est
=

26 advertise + ment
=

21 forbid + en
=

24 blot + er
=

Score one point for each correct answer.

Learn-by-heart spellings   Circle the correct version.

27 apology or appology

29 suprised or surprised

28 intrested or interested

30 gradually or gradully

SCORE

28

/ 30

ie or ei?

Here is a useful rhyme which will help you sort out most **ie** and **ei** words. You may know the first half but it's important to know it all.

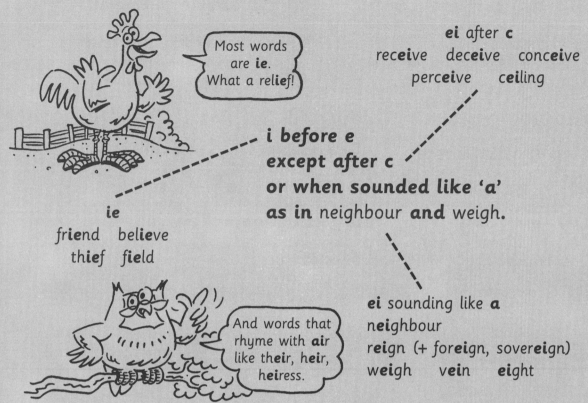

ei after **c**
rec**ei**ve   dec**ei**ve   conc**ei**ve
perc**ei**ve   c**ei**ling

Most words are **ie**. What a relief!

i before e
except after c
or when sounded like 'a'
as in neighbour **and** weigh.

ie
fr**ie**nd   bel**ie**ve
th**ie**f   f**ie**ld

And words that rhyme with **air** like th**ei**r, h**ei**r, h**ei**ress.

ei sounding like **a**
n**ei**ghbour
r**ei**gn (+ for**ei**gn, sover**ei**gn)
w**ei**gh   v**ei**n   **ei**ght

If you apply the rule carefully, you won't find many exceptions. If in doubt, check in a dictionary. These are the main exceptions:

either, neither, heifer, height, leisure, protein, seize, weir, weird

Apply the rule and get these right every time.

1	pr _ _ st	**6**	p _ _ r	**11**	rec _ _ pt
2	conc _ _ ted	**7**	r _ _ ndeer	**12**	w _ _ ght
3	n _ _ ghbourhood	**8**	dec _ _ t	**13**	shr _ _ k
4	br _ _ fcase	**9**	_ _ ghteen	**14**	w _ _ ghbridge
5	sh _ _ ld	**10**	n _ _ ce	**15**	h _ _ ress

■ TEST 5 ■

Revision

Give the plural.

1 butterfly _____

2 woman _____

3 knife _____

4 piano _____

Circle the correct spelling.

5 careful   carefull

6 forecast   forcast

7 onest   honest

8 finaly   finally

Supply the missing letter.

9 i _ formation

11 intellig _ nt

13 d _ scription

10 pro _ ably

12 sep _ rately

Use a prefix to make the meaning opposite.

14 certain   **15** agree   **16** understand   **17** visible

ie or ei?

18 fr _ _ ndly   **19** n _ _ ghbour   **20** conc _ _ ted

Do these word sums.

21 make + ing _____

23 forget + ful _____

22 marry + ed _____

24 sad + est _____

Choose the right word from the brackets.

25 We have eaten _____ much.   (to, too, two)

26 Do you _____ the time?   (know, no)

27 I can _____ your dog barking.   (hear, here)

Write the short form, using the apostrophe.

28 do not _____   **29** it has _____

30 they are _____

Score one point for each correct answer.

SCORE

30

30

Answers

Page 4
1 knife
2 plumber
3 neighbour
4 scissors
5 gnat
6 rhubarb
7 numb
8 design
9 straight
10 foreign
11 knock
12 wrong

Page 5
1 wren
2 guinea-pig
3 wrist
4 hymn
5 guest
6 pseudonym
7 guillotine
8 wreath

Page 7
1 were
2 to
3 no
4 to, your
5 here
6 It's
7 where, were
8 know, no
9 we're, we're
10 hear
11 know
12 where
13 were
14 They're
15 You're
16 It's
17 hear

TEST 1 Page 8
1 knife
2 scissors
3 debt

4 ghost
5 knee
6 science
7 knuckle
8 sign
9 muscle
10 honest
11 solemn
12 daughter
13 sword
14 write
15 guitar
16 receipt
17 wrist
18 guest
19 hymn
20 wreath
21 It's
22 too
23 were
24 They're
25 know
26 You're
27 hear
28 paid
29 among
30 perhaps

Page 9
1 can't
2 isn't
3 haven't
4 didn't
5 I'm, you're
6 should've
7 won't

Page 10
1 autobiography
2 antifreeze
3 telephone/
   microphone
4 interview
5 microwave
6 foretell
7 uncertain
8 misbehave

9 disagree
10 impolite
11 misdirect/
   indirect
12 unconscious
13 irreplaceable
14 disconnect
15 unhelpful

Page 11
1 kindness
2 friendly
3 existence
4 finally
5 joyful
6 sadness
7 especially
8 playfully
9 visible
10 grammar
11 sentence

TEST 2 Page 12
1 we've
2 they're
3 who's
4 aren't
5 don't
6 shan't
7 didn't
8 should've
9 I'll
10 it's
11 misunderstand
12 unknown
13 disapprove
14 illegible
15 disagree
16 impossible
17 misbehave
18 irregular
19 immediately
20 advertisement
21 forgetful
22 sullenness
23 wonderfully
24 visible

25 really
26 careful
27 keenness
28 excited
29 description
30 lonely

Page 13
1 pencils
2 addresses
3 crutches
4 blackboards
5 brushes
6 boxes
7 peaches
8 rulers
9 prefixes
10 princesses
11 arguments
12 sentences
13 suffixes
14 examinations
15 businesses
16 advertisements

Page 14
1 jockeys
2 monkeys
3 trolleys
4 birthdays
5 butterflies
6 babies
7 parties
8 lorries
9 robbery
10 alley
11 jelly
12 daisy
13 journey
14 memory
15 storeys
16 valleys
17 cries
18 bullies
19 allergies
20 donkeys

Page 15
1 tattoos
2 videos
3 tomatoes
4 studios
5 contraltos
6 potatoes
7 patios
8 echoes
9 cuckoos

Page 16
1 beliefs
2 roofs
3 wives
4 cuffs
5 loaves
6 hoofs/hooves
7 themselves
8 proofs
9 leaves
10 reefs

Page 17
1 hippopotamus
2 geese
3 cod
4 bacteria
5 louse
6 women
7 crises

TEST 3 Page 18
1 stations
2 telephones
3 crosses
4 matches
5 computers
6 stitches
7 hobbies
8 keys
9 centuries
10 memories
11 stories
12 storeys
13 discos
14 echoes

15 tomatoes
16 pianos
17 volcanoes
18 igloos
19 roofs
20 halves
21 beliefs
22 handkerchiefs
23 shelves
24 flagstaffs
25 children
26 deer
27 oases
28 mice
29 oxen
30 women

TEST 3 Page 19

1 foxes
2 wolves
3 lice
4 lynxes
5 trout
6 kangaroos
7 turkeys
8 walruses
9 canaries
10 lionesses
11 hens
12 ponies
13 wallabies
14 stags
15 geese
16 cockatoos
17 hoof
18 enemy
19 cargo
20 kimono
21 fungus
22 separately
23 immediately
24 scarcely
25 difficult
26 extremely
27 definitely
28 anxious
29 sincerely
30 annoyed

Page 20

1 snapping
2 sadden
3 funny
4 sadly
5 spotless
6 fretful

Page 21

1 dragging
2 rimless
3 winner
4 piglet
5 wrapper
6 sunny
7 scarred
8 droplet
9 snapped
10 patted
11 wetter
12 dimness
13 sadness
14 sadly
15 hotly

Page 22

1 making
2 famous
3 lazy
4 safely
5 sincerely
6 something
7 tiresome
8 exciting
9 valuable
10 announcement

Page 23

1 saviour
2 believable
3 writing
4 advertisement
5 decoration
6 careless
7 tuneful
8 pining
staring
riding
taped
sloping
scared
NB hopped, planning, scarred are 1-1-1 words.

Page 24

1 employment
2 delayed
3 betrayal
4 copier
5 beautiful
6 emptiness
7 fortieth
8 worrying

Page 25

1 funniest
2 terrifying
3 earlier
4 delaying
5 babyish
6 mysterious
7 denial
8 worried
9 laziest
10 playful
11 carrier
12 prayer
13 payment

Page 27

1 numberless
2 shatterproof
3 gossipmonger
4 riveting
5 difference
6 orbited
7 submitted
8 forbidden
9 equipping
10 parallelogram
11 equality
12 excellent
13 tranquillity

TEST 4 Page 28

1 hopping
2 hoping
3 sunny
4 madly
5 excitement
6 something
7 worried
8 noisily
9 obeying
10 various
11 twentieth
12 enjoyment
13 gossiped
14 regretful
15 committed
16 happening
17 follower
18 labelled
19 laziness
20 sloping
21 forbidden
22 hopeless
23 easiest
24 blotter
25 galloping
26 advertisement
27 apology
28 interested
29 surprised
30 gradually

Page 29

1 priest
2 conceited
3 neighbourhood
4 briefcase
5 shield
6 pier
7 reindeer
8 deceit
9 eighteen
10 niece
11 receipt
12 weight
13 shriek
14 weighbridge
15 heiress

TEST 5 Page 30

1 butterflies
2 women
3 knives
4 pianos
5 careful
6 forecast
7 honest
8 finally
9 information
10 probably
11 intelligent
12 separately
13 description
14 uncertain
15 disagree
16 misunderstand
17 invisible
18 friendly
19 neighbour
20 conceited
21 making
22 married
23 forgetful
24 saddest
25 too
26 know
27 hear
28 don't
29 it's
30 they're